ENCHANTING
INDIA

REETA & RUPINDER KHULLAR

ENCHANTING
INDIA

The Himalayas : The world's highest mountains

Coastal India : Where three seas meet

Nature and Wildlife :

Gods and Goddesses : Welcome to Hindu India

Architectural Traditions : A synthesis through ages

Royal Homes : Forts

Buddhist India : In the footsteps of Buddha

The Faces of India : People and their lifestyles

Kingdoms of Rajasthan : Princely India in the desert

Madhya Pradesh and Khajuraho

Mumbai :

Kolkata in the East : City of Joy

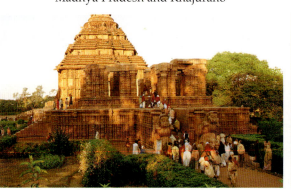
Sun spangled Orissa : Land of the Gods

The Secrets of Sikkim

fauna and flora

Festivals and Rituals : A land of celebration

Palaces in India

Crafts : The skill of the artisan

Delhi, Agra, Jaipur : The Golden Triangle

Portuguese Goa : India's playground by the sea

The Wonders of the South

Contents

Introduction	13
The Himalayas The world's highest mountains	22
Coastal India Where three seas meet	28
Nature and Wildlife Rare fauna and flora	36
Festivals and Rituals A land of celebration	42
Gods and Goddesses Welcome to Hindu India	50
Architectural Traditions A synthesis through ages	58
Royal Homes Forts and Palaces in India	68
Crafts The skill of the artisan	74
Buddhist India In the footsteps of the Buddha	78
The Faces of India People and their lifestyles	84
Delhi, Agra, Jaipur The Golden Triangle	92
Kingdoms of Rajasthan Princely India in the desert	100
Madhya Pradesh and Khajuraho Exploring the heart of India	106
Mumbai The city of West	110
Portuguese Goa India's playground by the sea	114
Kolkata in the East City of Joy	118
Sun spangled Orissa Land of the Gods	122
The Secrets of Sikkim Himalayan fastnesses	126
The Wonders of the South Discovering spirit of ancient India	130

Landscapes, building, people, art, all come together in kaleidoscopic India. pp 2-3, palm-fringed coast; pp 6-7, Kolkata's distinctive Victoria Memorial; pp 8-9, idyllic scene from Himalayan Kashmir; pp 10-11, dressed in their finery, women celebrate the Bat-kamma festival in Andhra Pradesh.
This page: spectacular mask and costume mark the ancient dance drama form of Kathakali from Kerala.

INTRODUCTION

India it is just a word, but it communicates so much more. At once, a civilisation that is five thousand years old, and a country that is at the frontiers of the knowledge revolution. Once, and not so long ago, it was considered a mysterious land, a place in the far reaches of myth, a remote part of the world where tigers and elephants, or so believed people in other equally distant lands, walked the streets among the strange tribes that inhabited her.

It was galling for many Indians, for India—newly independent from the yoke of colonial rule—had chosen a socialist pattern of governance to try and raise the nation from its appalling poverty to an era of prosperity. It was a period when India was cut off, metaphorically, if not literally, from the world. In the decades that it struggled to found solutions within its democratic framework, India was often ignored in the world of ideas.

The last decades have changed that. Today, India is fashionable globally. Its food and its films and its fashion have found favour around the world. Its tryst with destiny—which its first prime minister, Jawaharlal Nehru had promised at the time of independence from British rule—has begun. As a nuclear power, it found respect (and, admittedly, fear) among the world's leader nations, but even as it has liberalized and brought in economic reforms that are changing its perception as a market, Indians—for long caricatured in Hollywood cinema—have changed the very notion of nationhood. Just as the Western world had used the industrial revolution to create riches for itself, India has rapidly risen up the ladder of global success using information technology to empower itself. Today, when the world looks to India, it is to find a rapidly changing country that is integrating social change into its very fabric of life.

It is not to say that the face of India—its ancient allure and its medieval marvels—are any less visible. In rapidly changing urbanscapes and regenerating infrastructure, India is reinventing itself. But the reasons the world makes a reservation to come discover her mysterious secrets, are no less impressive.

Yes, for those who will make the time, there are both elephants and tigers, to be found in her national parks, as also other rare species of animals (the Asiatic lion, the one-horned rhinoceros, the Hoolock gibbon, the spotted leopard, a variety of deer, wild boar and bison among them) and reptiles (the gharial or Indian river crocodile, snatched from extinction, the fierce cobra) and among the largest variety of birds ever in a single country.

And yes, there are beautifully carved temples from the medieval ages, forts as ancient as history and palaces as stupendous as fairytales. In a country that has the second-largest population (over a billion people) in the world, there are people of many races and vintage—the Dravidians, who some historians believe were the original settlers who created the five-thousand-year-old riverine settlement of the Indus Valley Civilization, the martial Aryans who created the India of its many gods and its many rituals, the tribals who live in her deep forests and distant islands, some now part of mainstream life, others living gypsy existences, still others so isolated they're still part of the stone age.

Here, in lands lush with forests, watered by many rivers, crowned by the Himalayas, flanked by deserts and oceans, dotted by islands, civilizations grew, flourished, vanished. But they left their imprints behind, not just in the land but also in the region. As the cradle of many of the world's religions—Hinduism (though it is said it is less a religion more a way of living),

Buddhism, Jainism, Sikhism—the country was receptive to other religious ideas. Christianity was quick to travel to this land of sages and philosophers, and found acceptance. Islam followed. Zoroastrianism took root. Even the Jews, facing persecution in many parts of the world, sought sanctuary and flourished in India.

In the melee of the land, it was difficult not to be absorbed. Over millennia, people have travelled to India for different reasons. The ancient Chinese and the medieval Europeans came in search of learning and knowledge, to travel through her many kingdoms recording what they saw, ancient scribes who took the idea of India to their own countries. Wandering tribes came to settle, but many also came as invaders—to pillage her legendary riches. They carried back tales of enormous wealth, of fabulous precious stones and rare silks, of spices and incense.

By ship and in caravans, they came to trade, to settle, perhaps even to rule. Here, in India, there were already sophisticated systems of business in place. The distinctive caste system—so abhorred in modern society—was then a means to ensure a disciplined society. The priests provided the essential link with the gods and were the guiding force on earth; the warrior rulers would guard their lands though rarely start wars to usurp other lands; the traders kept society on a roll; and the artisans used their skills to create the objects that, even now (as family-knit groups descended from the same ateliers), keep the country supplied with its excellent handwoven textiles, its handicrafts, its paintings and sculpture and jewellery: as beautifully executed now as it has been for generations before theirs.

India. A loose confederation that was an idea called Bharatvarsh—the land of Bharat, who ruled here, as the legend goes, many millennia ago. Under the Mauryan dynasty that reigned from Pataliputra (where India is today), much of it did come under their sway. The Mughals too united vastly disparate provinces to make their empire among the largest the world had seen. But, for most part, through centuries, under various dynasties, India was never one, but a huge cauldron of kingdoms big and small. It knew periods of peace and eras of strife. If there were internecine battles, there were also mercenaries from Europe who came to make use of their superior training in firearms, to lead armies one against the other. This was Hindustan—not, as is assumed, the land of the Hindus, but the settlers who assumed the name of the life-giving river that emerged from the Himalayas—the Indus.

But the land of the Indus had many other rivers too, rivers as much a part of its myth as of history and geography. There was the Ganga, the most sacred of rivers in the world, descended, so it is believed, from the very heavens. Along her course cities were raised and razed. Delhi— once the ancient city of the Pandavas (then known as Indraprastha)— where the heros of that epic ruled before their cousins, the Kauravas, declared war upon them.

But Delhi was destined to rule, and it did as different dynasties occupied it, leaving behind remnants of their reign over its hardy scrub by way of walled settlements, iron pillar edicts, victory towers, mosques, tombs, water tanks, forts and palaces. It remains, still, the seat of power for the government of India, after the British, who first occupied Calcutta (now renamed Kolkata) and made it their imperial capital, also decided that its central, strategic position was more suited to its role of governance of a huge land—practically a continent itself.

But other cities grew along the banks of the Ganga. Allahabad, a city of learning; Patna, where the ancient Mauryans had their capital; Benares (or Varanasi), probably the world's oldest living city, and sacred to Hinduism, for this is where, they believe, to die is to escape the endless chain of rebirths and find eternal moksha; and Kolkata itself, where the Ganga is known as the Hooghly, and which, not so long ago, was the brightest outpost of Empire.

There is also the Brahmaputra, a huge, gawping maw of a river that is brown with silt as it moves through India's east, feeding estuaries of the Bengal flood lands as it descends into neighbouring country Bangladesh to disappear into the Bay of Bengal. And the Narmada, which has attracted much world attention in recent times for the dam being built on the river that created a huge environmental and human resettlement issue. The dam has been built, villagers have been displaced, but its success is still to be measured in Madhya Pradesh and Gujarat, the two states whose fortunes it most affects, before spilling into the Arabian Sea on India's west coast.

Many other rivers are a part of India's landscape—the Godavari in the South, Jhelum in Kashmir, the five rivers of Punjab from which it takes its name—but little has excited the Indian imagination as much as the Saraswati, the river of learning, mentioned in old religious texts. Today, though, the river no longer exists, even though towns and settlements mentioned in the texts, continue to survive. Where did the river disappear? Did it ever exist? Was it always an allegorical myth? The Saraswati was the legendary river that gave birth to the prosperous civilizations of Harappa and Mohenjodaro, many of which have been excavated to show urban settlements with great baths, harbours, and modern city planning. And along with the Ganga and the Yamuna, it is the third (if now missing) river that meets at the confluence called Sangam, where Allahabad, that ancient seat of learning and modern education, was established. Here, every twelve years, the largest congregation of people takes place, at the Kumbha Mela, when saints and sages, holy men and god men, and millions of those with just faith, or curiosity, gather to bathe in the river, seek salvation or lessons in spirituality. But the Mela, or fair, is also an annual event, no less fantastic for that, even though the venue changes to some other spots—Haridwar in the Himalayan foothills of Uttaranchal, and in the states of Madhya Pradesh and Maharashtra.

If the Saraswati river disappeared (and geo-satellite mapping efforts are on to see if it did, in fact, exist; though currently there has been little to show by way of positive results), so did the people who lived in these towns and cities four and five thousand years ago. Who were these people and why did they suddenly abandon their settlements spread thousands of kilometers apart? There are no answers, for the script of those of the Indus Valley civilization has still to be deciphered—one of the last true mysteries of the modern world. But for the moment, ancient India has chosen to keep her secrets.

But legends, as they often do, are often based on truth, no matter how hazy. Off the coast of Gujarat, in Dwarka, the city where India's most playful god, Krishna, came to rule and eventually die, scientists have now found the remnants of an old city—not unlike Atlantis. Is this Krishna's city? Was Krishna then a historical figure? In Mathura and Brindavan, close to the Taj Mahal in Agra, where he was born and spent his childhood and adolescence, his myth has been kept alive not just in the numerous temples dedicated to him but also in cultural associations. Krishna and his beloved consort Radha (and not his wife Rukmini) are celebrated in dance and in painting, and are the basis for a large number of resonances that are part of India's artscape. (More recently, the tsunami that devastated parts of Asia and lashed India, saw the sea recede from Mahabalipuram on Tamil Nadu's southern coast, to deposit granite rock-cut sculpture on its shore, lending credence to the legend of the seven pagodas that were once said to be here.)

But then, art has often been inspired by its religions and its myths. For generations, sculptors have carved tales from the Mahabharata and the Ramayana—India's most popular and the world's longest epics—their tales have been painted and enacted, told in pantomimes and re-told in theatre. The resonances of these myths and their artistic legacy have survived to most part in India, but they have also left behind deep impressions in South-east Asia where, from temples and sculpture to dance forms, are still enacted the tales of the model king Rama and his virtuous wife Sita, or of the clash of the warring Pandava and Kaurava brothers on account of the vengeful Draupadi, wife of the five Pandava siblings. Alongside, Buddhism too travelled to the South-east and Far East, and even to distant Afghanistan in the north-west frontier, but increasingly under the Muslim rule in Delhi, saints and seers, poets and writers from West Asia established links with India, creating Sufi philosophy and poetry, now enjoying a resurgence with its message of peace and harmony.

India's Muslim rulers were settlers; its colonial settlers were migrants. While the British controlled most of India in the eighteenth and nineteenth centuries, the Portuguese and the French and the Dutch too occupied pockets, bent on leaching it of its riches. Europe prospered on her colonies, not least of which was India. And when the British left India, in a final act of humiliation, they divided the nation, creating Pakistan on its western and eastern flanks. It was an act of great tragedy, for it unleashed one of the largest migrations in history that led to bloodshed on a scale that could not have been imagined. Almost a quarter of a century later, East Pakistan became independent as Bangladesh, but both India and Pakistan are still coming to terms with an uneasy recent history as they strive to make sense of borders and boundaries and territories over which they have fought three wars, and now walk the narrow path to an uneasy peace.

Even though Pakistan was created as Muslim nation, secular India has retained most of its Islamic legacy—whether by way of its distinctive Mughlai cuisine, its fabulous craftsmen, as well as its architectural wonders that include first and foremost the world's most pristine monument, the flawless Taj Mahal in Agra. But remnants of the Khilji, Slave and Mughal dynasties are evident throughout much of India—the forts in Delhi and Agra, the Qutab Minar and Humayun's Tomb in Delhi, the Itmad-ud-Daulah and Fatehpur Sikri in Agra, the Imambaras of Lucknow, the great palaces and Golconda in Hyderabad, the gardens of Tipu Sultan in Karnataka, the Bibi-ka-Maqbara in Aurangabad, in Maharashtra. In time to come, a blend of Islamic, Hindu and European architecture would create a new—and truly incredible—synthesis in what has since some to be known as the Indo-Saracenic style, of which New Delhi's Rashtrapati Bhawan is a premier example. But India's cities—Bombay and Calcutta in particular—are virtual museums of Elizabethan, Gothic, Regency and Art Deco architecture, much of it still extant.

Indeed, if anything, India's architectural legacy alone is truly monumental. From cave paintings in the forested heartlands of the country, to the Ajanta and Ellora Caves where monks meditated in rock-cut temples of immense size, painted with frescos and chiselled into brilliant sculpture, to the erotic temples of tenth and eleventh century Khajuraho; from Buddhist monasteries tucked into the remote fastnesses of the Himalayas to the gilded Golden Temple of the Sikhs; from terracotta temples in Bengal to the grand forts of Rajasthan, India is a journey of many contrasts, but linked by a heritage of common synthesis of religion, culture and architecture.

Imagine, if you will, a train journey across India. You will cross many bridges over several rivers and streams, for hours the eyes will be mesmerized by its huge plains sweltering under a bright sun, producing among the world's largest quantities of grain, and the greatest quantity of fruit. If India's "green" revolution has been successful into turning the vast land into a huge granary, its "white" revolution (also referred to as Operation Flood) has been successful in making the country both self-sufficient as well as the largest producer of milk and dairy products in the world. Traversing the Himalayas, past its Gangetic plains, through deep forests, across deserts and flood estuaries, across rocky foothills and the great Ghats, through paddy fields, by sea coasts, it would be an incredible journey over many days, climates and cultures, where everything from the cuisine to the clothes and the language changes frequently. Truly, there is unity in diversity, and you have to be in India to know diversity.

India, at once ancient and modern. For its vast masses that still live in the countryside, the challenge has been to provide equal opportunities and amenities to both its rural and urban sectors. This is by no means an easy task. A government strapped for funds, finds itself seeking to provide education for all children, besides running adult literacy programmes; to usher in gender equality and representation at grassroots levels through participation in the political process. Where water is scarce (women walk for miles altogether in Rajasthan to fetch water from wells), electricity still not available in all villages and hamlets, it is an uphill task, but slowly, India is transforming herself. It is the reason education is given such a high priority—the chance for even the most backward and poor to enter the mainstream of life, and rub shoulders with their better-educated fellow-Indians.

But even as India is undergoing gigantic changes—though there is still abysmal poverty, and a huge infrastructure remains to be built—the world, it appears, cannot get enough of India. For some time now, India has been the flavour of the world. Its food, for starters, has become hugely popular, and Indian restaurants are trendy in Europe and the United States of America, across Asia and even in China. (And just for the record, Indian beers are doing quite well outside the country; and its wine industry, though still in its infancy, is showing great promise and will soon take its place in a sommelier's list of New World wines.)

Indian food—what is it to you? For, within the country itself, the variety is so huge and so distinctive, that people from one region find the food of any other region alien. With the exception of a few staples such as dal (lentils) or the flat breads that accompany most meals, there is no standardization, providing a huge gastronomic board that even Indians never tire of experimenting with. The majority of Indians are vegetarians (that is, they will eat nothing that has any animal product used in the process of cooking; the reasons are more social, and religious, than health-driven). While the non-vegetarian percentage is small, the number of such diners and their variety of food are immense. (And here, it must be pointed out, that there are communities, such as the Jains and the Maheshwaris, who as vegetarians, do not consume root vegetables, garlic and onions and chillies, so as not to stimulate the senses.) But equally, for the visitor, it is confusing: Hindus will not eat beef, Muslims will not touch pork, fish and seafood is not a north-Indian favourite, chicken is consumed in huge quantities in Punjab and the north, lamb is preferred. (It would require a brave man to invite an Indian home for a meal, given all these constraints!) With a ban on hunting, almost all game has disappeared from the menu, though farm-bred quail or partridge and rabbit are exceptions. But from the spices to the gravies (there is no such thing as a "curry" dish; it is a Western misnomer for Indian food), food is cooked differently not only within each state, but practically within each region (and that changes every hundred kilometers or so!).

While Indian gourmet restaurants are much sought after overseas as, of course, in India (and you can carry back packaged Indian foods), you will not find India short of international cuisines and restaurants. In the cities, urban trends dictate current world favourites. There are fusion restaurants and lounge, bed and Buddha bars. As elsewhere, Mediterranean, Middle Eastern and other cuisines are enjoying a burst of popularity, though staple favourites over the years that have established themselves firmly on the Indian palate include Italian, Chinese, Thai, European (as opposed to classic French), even Japanese (sushi is becoming the rage here). In cities, "spice" or South-east Asian restaurants offer a mélange of cuisines that range from coastal southern India to Singapore, China, Thailand, Hong Kong, Malaysia, Cambodia and so on.

As in cuisine, so in fashion. Indian fashion has begun to go global, and the industry is now thriving on its haute couture, diffusion and prêt lines. At important events such as beauty pageants, the Oscars and Grammys, the stars are now turning to Indian designers to dress them up. Equally, the jewellery they sport is most likely to have come from Indian design houses (but then, India is the largest processor of diamonds in the world, and its largest centre for gem cutting and polishing).

More interestingly, it is Western designers who continue to seek their inspiration from India, and which has now embedded itself on to their consciousness. Of course, a large number of them outsource work to India, but they include embellishments (think beads, embroidery, sequins), textiles (most still hand-woven or hand block printed according to traditional designs and motifs) and inspiration. India on the ramp is blazing and alive.

As is Indian cinema. The world's largest producer of films (some 800 annually), the "Bollywood" genre, as Hindi cinema has come to be represented, is now keenly watched around the world. Not only is it a powerful means of entertainment for the millions of non-resident Indians and people of Indian origin, but is as keenly viewed by people from different cultures. More recently, of course, international stars have started seeking roles in Hindi (and the various regional language offshoots) cinema, but equally, Indian stars are sought after for Hollywood productions.

If Indian cinema is all extravaganza, an attempt at serious or parallel cinema has given rise to several new genres that do well in India's multiplexes as well as on overseas screens. Equally importantly, India is being used as a cinematic hub, and with its cost savings, could offer the best facilities for making global cinema. Already, animation films are being made in India, or are being outsourced here, and this is continuing to increase as better technologies and cheaper options become available.

Indian theatre extravaganzas have started storming Broadway. Indian stars, epics, shows and themes are opening up a mine of opportunities, and with Indian bands and underground music becoming big in London, Indian musical beats, experimentation and medleys are rocking the world of music.

With the economy opening up, India's beautiful women are walking the ramp with international designers, but in the last decade, several Indian women have also walked off with the crowns at international beauty pageants. In the West, yoga is a huge industry, and workshops attract thousands to this Indian way of meditation and exercise, to its sense of wellness and well being.

All of this is not to point away from India's many problems. Yet, the airports are being modernized, an open-sky policy has suddenly given rise to a large number of private carriers on both the domestic and international routes so India is no longer inaccessible, or difficult (or even expensive) to travel around in. And though it has several international hotel chains, and several Indian chains of international quality, there is suddenly a huge pressure on the availability of rooms. This, too, should soon be sorted out, for millions around the world have decided to join in the journey to India.

It is true that India assaults your senses. It is equally true that it comes as a shock. So many people! So many colours! So much poverty! So much richness! Most love it. Some hate it. Nobody is indifferent to it.

For visitors, the experience—packaged as it is most likely to be—will never be sterile. In all possibility, it will include what is known as the Golden Triangle (Delhi, with its seven ancient cities, and now its eighth, as a flourishing, national capital; Agra, with its exquisite Taj Mahal, the world's most perfectly proportionate building, but also with other forts and monuments around it; and Jaipur, the provincial capital of the state of Rajasthan, elegantly grand and nostalgically royal). But the cultural circuit also includes other segments. On the one side, this is Mumbai (the new name for Bombay, and the country's financial capital), Aurangabad (which is the base for visiting the rock-cut caves of Ajanta and Ellora, one of the most awe-inspiring wonders of the ancient world, with sculptures and paintings preserved in caves that have been shaped and patterned like gigantic temples), Udaipur (Rajasthan's lake city with fairytale-like palaces and forts) and Jodhpur (a rugged, desert kingdom with an awesome fort atop a hill). On another side, this would include Khajuraho (medieval temple town with facades completely covered with sculpture, including erotic details), Banaras (India's holiest city, and its most ancient, on the banks of the Ganga), Bhubaneswar (capital of Orissa, also celebrated for its medieval temples) and Kolkata (formerly Calcutta, capital of the British Raj, and now known as City of Joy based on writer Dominique Lapierre's book—made into a film—on life and survival in its slums).

Of course, this is only the tip of the iceberg. Imagine, if you will, once important kingdoms, each of which had its own architectural and natural marvels. Under British occupation, while many of the kingdoms acknowledged overall British suzerainty, the rest became British-governed India. At the time of independence (bitterly won, with Britain finally subjugated by the non-violent path of non-cooperation that was exercised by Mahatma Gandhi), the states were merged into independent India on the basis of a roughly drawn out regional and vernacular heritage (India has eighteen languages recognized by its Constitution, and hundreds of dialects). As a result, for years after, the states continued to be reorganized (and indeed, have been till recently). The government, therefore, functions at two levels – at the state level, and as a centre, resulting in a boisterous, noisy democracy—the world's largest. For India, it is a matter of pride that not only has democracy proved successful, its systems – such as the electronic voting machines – have been observed, and are now being emulated, by so-called first world countries!

While north India was better known to tourists for decades, the southern part has been a slow starter, but Kerala has taken the lead in providing some of the most memorable holidays for people. Karnataka, capital Bangalore, once India's "garden city", is now known as the country's Silicon Valley. It has become the major centre for information technology companies from around the globe, while for the young professionals who seek employment in this new avenue, it has been for long the country's "pub capital".

Once part of Mysore kingdom (located a two-hour drive away, with a huge confection of a palace), it has the ancient Vijaynagar empire ruins in Hampi as a major attraction. Kerala, of course, is known for its backwaters and gentle towns with their mixed Hindu and Muslim and Christian, Indian, Chinese and West Asian influences. The south's two other states are Tamil Nadu, with its capital Chennai (earlier Madras), and Andhra Pradesh with its capital Hyderbad (once part of the royal, and usually estranged Deccan) increasingly known as Cyberabad because of its rapid growth as an IT centre.

On the western coast, inching up, there's Goa, India's famed (and extremely popular) beach country—a forever holiday destination with a strong Portuguese tradition of Christianity, churches and cuisine. Maharashatra (and its spectacular Ghats, vast ranges of hills with the sea on one side and fertile soil on the other, over which the warrior-king Shivaji once ruled) make way for the arid scrubland of Gujarat (and its royal kingdoms, both Hindu and Muslim) before finally giving way to Rajasthan, covered by the Thar, the land of the fierce Rajputs, who once reigned over 20 kingdoms here (another two were the domain of Jat and Muslim rulers).

Glance at the Himalayas on top, and in a moment you can see the mountainous states that separate it from Pakistan, China and Nepal. There's Jammu and Kashmir consisting of three distinct regions – the cold mountain desert of Ladakh and its Buddhist monasteries; the Muslim dominated Kashmir valley with its enchanting lakes, often referred to as the Swizerland of the East; and Jammu, with its Hindu temples and gentle hills.

The state of Himachal Pradesh may be small, but it is spectacular, and its provincial capital, Shimla, was once the summer capital of the British Raj. One of the most popular summer destinations for Indian tourists, the whole state is dominated by oak and conifer forests, and is snow covered in the higher ranges, as also is Uttaranchal (with its districts of Garhwal, with Mussoorie as its centre, and Kumaon, with Nainital as its base).

Bits of Bengal also range up to the Himalayas (think Darjeeling) and much of this region, as well as the foothills of Assam are part of India's famous tea country. Seven small states make up North-east India (and are known as its Seven Sisters), with a distinctive culture, isolated from the rest of India because of the geographical terrain that consists of dense forests and rolling hills. These include Sikkim (fabulous trekking trails and Buddhist monasteries), Meghalaya (with its matrilineal society, and its capital referred to as the Scotland of the East), Nagaland, Manipur, Arunachal Pradesh, Mizoram and Tripura.

With such a vast geographical, historical and cultural legacy, it's hardly any wonder that festivals are observed almost on a daily basis in some part of the country or another. Some of the larger, and more national in character, are festivals such as Diwali (the autumn festival of lights and of firecrackers) and Holi (the spring festival of colours), as well as Dussehra (also known as Durga Puja, and celebrated so differently in Delhi and Kullu, in Mysore and Kolkata). But there are Sikh and Buddhist and Christian feasts, Hindu celebrations and Islamic ones. And then, there are regional fairs that have been held for so long, no one knows their origins. The Pushkar fair in Rajasthan is one such, where hundreds of thousands of people come to buy and sell camels (and horses), to have a holy bath in Pushkar lake, and to meet friends and relatives (and solemnize marriages). In Sonepur, in distant Bihar, the largest cattle fair in the world is held. Social, religious or commercial reasons bring together vast swathes of people, and in India you can travel from fair to festival to feast for every day of your life, and still not experience them all!

For those visitors who take the time to read through its newspapers, a puzzling phenomenon might be the "matrimonial" sections, which devote several score pages each weekend to matchmaking. Advertisements request alliances for marriages between young people based on religion and caste, a matching of horoscopes (based on planetary ascendants and descendants), social placement and the nature of jobs held. In a sense, this is like the Western dating system, only supervised by elders in the family, who accept this as a part of their responsibility. It is not unusual for prospective brides and grooms to never have met; increasingly, though, they are now allowed to meet for brief periods before agreeing to a match. "Love" marriages are still a rarity, and limited to the cities, and are ever so slightly looked down upon condescendingly.

Such elaborate arrangements are because families in India still live together, and though urban jobs have put an end to the former, even in cities it is the norm for grown-up sons and their parents to live together (making some form of compromise between them necessary). This is less to do with financial constraints but more to do with a sense of respect – after all, families are meant to stay together, and nothing can change that.

In a sense, though this has built a support system for the aged and the young to live together, in recent decades it has given rise to a growing social menace, the system of dowry – the woman's share of her parents' property, that is now "demanded" by grooms and their families. Brides that do not bring appropriate dowries are hassled, harassed and even "accidentally burned" in a growing social horror. Government and police intervention, and television, might put an end to it, but this is still some while away.

Indian weddings themselves are great extravaganzas. Families spend a fortune in laying out lavish weddings, for grand feasts, numerous rituals and events, for invitations, costumes and clothes and finery, for decoration and music and entertainment. Such weddings can last for several days, are festive and entertaining. The groom comes on a horse (sometimes an elephant), the bride is coy and even tearful (she's leaving her natal home and is being given away to a stranger). Hordes of relatives and friends congregate and eat together, dance, have fun. Brides dress up in sequined gowns and veils, grooms in long tunics, resembling the maharajas and maharanis who once ruled over their kingdoms.

This sense of celebration and joie de vivre, of erudition (Indians can be argumentative) and learning, of tradition and culture and an acceptance of the new, all come together to make an India that is truly captivating and enchanting.

And yes, we do occasionally have camels and cattle and elephants on the road (you can spot them at red lights, right next to your luxury car or coach), but no, if you want to see our tigers, you'll have to head for the nearest zoo, or national park.

The Himalayas
The world's highest mountains

The world's highest mountain range is also its youngest—only 80 million years old—and still being formed, with a rise of three to four inches a year. This cosmic timelessness permeates all our perceptions of the majestic range, which is revered as the Abode of the Snows and of the Gods. Where else would you find fourteen summits stretching 8,000 metres (26,000 ft.) skywards, as if raising their hands to divinity? The sacred peak of Kailash (in Tibet) is the very centre of the universe, says Hindu belief; no wonder, then, that the life-giving waters of the mighty Brahmaputra flowed east from its snowy ridges, as did those of the Indus to the west.

A complex of ranges, such as the Pir Panjal, the Dhaula Dhar, the Zanskar, runs across India from Kashmir to Assam, enfolding a rich variety of eco-systems in the lower reaches. From the high-altitude desert of Ladakh in the west to the almost tropical lushness of the eastern Himalaya, the scenery encompasses everything from stark moonscapes to dense forests of pine and fir. And in the sunset, when the light has fired the snow with molten gold, you can believe the words of the Skanda Purana: 'As the sun dries the morning dew so does the mere sight of the Himalaya dissipate the sins of man.'

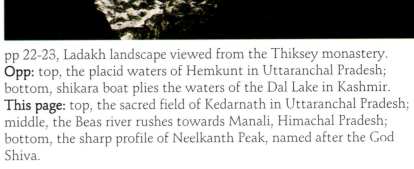

pp 22-23, Ladakh landscape viewed from the Thiksey monastery.
Opp: top, the placid waters of Hemkunt in Uttaranchal Pradesh; bottom, shikara boat plies the waters of the Dal Lake in Kashmir.
This page: top, the sacred field of Kedarnath in Uttaranchal Pradesh; middle, the Beas river rushes towards Manali, Himachal Pradesh; bottom, the sharp profile of Neelkanth Peak, named after the God Shiva.

Opp: top, emerald terraces seen en route to Nainital in Uttaranchal Pradesh; below, Nagar village in Himachal Pradesh.
This page: cottages in Gulmarg, Kashmir

Coastal India
Where three seas meet

To the ancient Indians Varuna was the God of the seas and oceans. They deified him as '... sovereign of the sea, (who) knows the ships thereon.' This reflects both the age-old maritime tradition of the country and its 7,500-kilometre-long sea coast caused by the thrust of the peninsula into the Indian Ocean—almost exactly half its land frontiers. The very names of the coasts spell romance—Coromandel, Konkan, Malabar. Off this vast coastline are two island strings surrounded by turquoise waters and beautiful coral reefs. To the west are the Lakshadweep Islands; to the east, the Andaman and Nicobar Islands about a thousand kilometres east of Kolkata.

Such length and variety give India countless beaches set in rich marinescapes: tranquil lagoons and backwaters, marine estuaries teeming with fish, bays and rough lava-rocked seas, crashing surf and golden sands fringed by swaying palms. Resorts abound on both coasts, from where cultures and cuisines differ from Gujarat and Konkan in the west to Orissa and the Sunderbans in the east. Not only is there abundant seafood to choose from but also an array of water sports from scuba to snorkelling, and spas where the ayurvedic oil massages are as relaxing as the soothing murmur of the tides.

pp 28-29, golden sands and turquoise waters reflect the serene charm of the Fort Aguada Beach Resort, Goa.
Opp: top, fishing boats are usually as simple as the one seen here while larger trawlers go further out into the sea; below, fish seller trudges the beach on the way to market.
This page: freshly-caught fish glisten in their baskets near Colva beach, Goa. They will soon be snapped up by eager buyers.

Opp: top, bright pink fishing nets make a colourful foreground in Ezhimala, Kerala; bottom, fish being placed to dry in Visakhapattnam, Andhra Pradesh.
This page: Slender coconut palms fringe Arambol beach in North Goa; middle, dramatic sea-sculpted rock, Arambol; bottom, sunrise at Kanya Kumari.

Opp: thatch-covered boat in the still backwaters of Kuttanad, Kerala.
This page: Dawn fires the sky at Havelock Island, Andaman and Nicobar.

Nature and Wildlife
Rare fauna and flora

'O Mother Earth,' says a hymn of the ancient Sanskrit scripture, the Atharva Veda, 'may I always replenish that which I take from thee.' Respect for nature and wildlife has been part of the Indian ethos since ancient times. Contained within her varied geography, India has an abundance of nurturing habitats such as rainforests, swamps, leafy glades, mangroves, scrub, desert, sub-montane areas and snow-capped mountains; in turn, these shelter countless species of plant, animal and bird life. More than 70 National Parks and about 400 wildlife sanctuaries continue to conserve this rich natural heritage.

Of mammals alone there are 350 species. Certainly the most famous is the tiger, which is also India's national animal; and if you are lucky, you may glimpse one in parks like Kanha or Corbett. If you go to Manas or Kaziranga in the east, you are likely to spot the one-horned rhinoceros; India harbours 80 per cent of the world's entire population of this animal. Areas such as Namdapha in Arunachal Pradesh and Silent Valley in Kerala are treasurehouses of biodiversity, where new plant and animal species are being discovered even today. Surely this irreplaceable legacy of nature's bounty is one to be respectfully admired and cherished for generations to come.

An abundance of habitats and wild life mark India's diverse geography, seen in the range of flora (pp 36-37), the ecstatic dance of the peacocks (pp 38-39); and the variety of animal and bird life.
Big cats include the tiger (opp: top left and this page: left) and the lion (opp: bottom left). India is home to the one-horned rhinoceros (opp: middle). Elephants (centre: top) are found in several states.
Wetlands shelter pelicans and herons (centre: middle and this page top right).

Festivals and Rituals
A land of celebration

There are said to be more festivals in India than there are days of the year. This may well be true, since the occasions of rituals and feasting spring from more than one reason. They may be spiritual in origin, moments of commemoration of the birth and great deeds of gods, goddesses, gurus, prophets and saints. They may be agricultural, a celebration of life and the bounty of nature after the harvest has been gathered and there is money to spend. Or they may follow the ordained calendar of the cosmos, the waxing and waning of the moon, or the entry of the sun into Capricorn which is a day marked by the flying of colourful kites.

Each of India's many religious groups—Hindus, Muslims, Christians, Sikhs, Buddhists, Jains, Parsis, and others—has its own such days. The spirit and colour of these religious or seasonal festivals draw people together, for Indians believe in sharing happiness. The whole neighborhood participates in such occasions, marked by sharing sweets and visiting family and friends. Thus, all communities join together for the joyous lights of Diwali, the blessings of Christmas, the birth of Guru Nanak and the bowls of sweetened vermicelli that mark the happiness of Id.

42

Fairs and festivals bring together spectacle, decoration and the whole-hearted participation of people.
pp 42-43, the famed snake boats seen during Onam in Kerala.
Opp: top, a cattle race in progress churns up mud; bottom, devotees throng to a procession during the Chitrai festival in Tamil Nadu.
This page: top, Jallikuttu, the thrill of bull running;
bottom, illuminated tank during the float festival, Madurai.

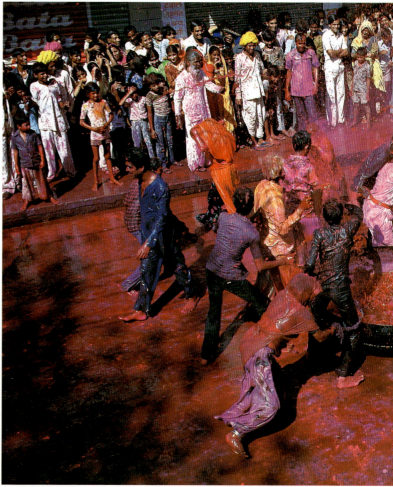

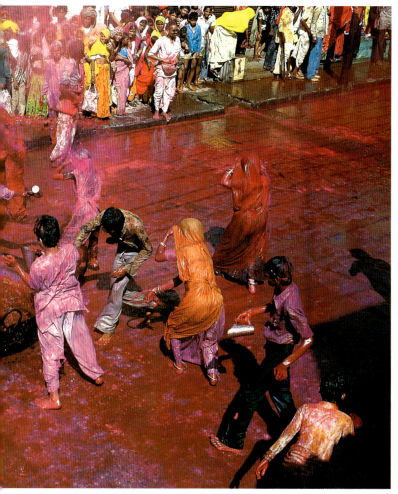

Opp: top left, King Momo's procession during the Goa Carnival; bottom left, the ghats at Banaras where the devout flock for a holy dip; top right, colour marks the spring festival of Holi; bottom right, Lamps glow during the evening prayers at Haridwar.

This page, top right, pilgrims make for the sanctum sanctorum of the Golden Temple, Amritsar; left, effigies of demons await burning on the final day of the autumn festival of Dussehra; above, Buddhist monks observe a festival at Sarnath.

Opp: top, devotees throng the Shri Mahavirji Jain temple during a religious fair; bottom, elephants arrayed in a magnificent spectacle for the Pooram festival of Trichur, Kerala.
This page: top, the Muslim festival of Id being celebrated at the Hawa Mahal in Jaipur; bottom, henna-decorated palms for the monsoon festival of Teej.

Gods and Goddesses
Welcome to Hindu India

Hinduism is many things to many people. It is the sweeping hymns of the Rig Veda, the searching quest of the Upanishads, the message of love and hope of the Bhagavad Gita. It is acceptance of, and adherence to, Dharma, the rule of good conduct and Karma, the law of causative justice. Equally, it is the millions of gods who illuminate our everyday lives, the familiar rituals of temple and home, the stories of valour, sacrifice and faith from the great epics. Above all, it is Santana Dharma, a faith so timeless that it has no beginning and no end and that will survive forever.

The one Supreme God is Brahman, Who is everywhere and in all things. But in our humanity we seek Him in many deities who are but His multiple faces. Thus our worship of Ganesh who makes all things auspicious, Shiva whose third eye scorches ignorance into ash and Durga who gives us the encompassing love of a mother. They are the tangible reminders we cling to in our striving for salvation from rebirth, so that we can achieve moksh and realise the immortal words of the Upanishads: 'From Joy we are come, and unto Joy shall we return'.

pp 50-51, students at a traditional Vedic school in Tamil Nadu. These pages: visual and iconic representations of the Divine Principle usually follow a time-tested regional vocabulary. Images, whether sculpted or painted, are richly dressed, bejewelled and garlanded with flowers preparatory to worship or processions.
Opp: top, deities, Mahamakham festival, Kumbhakonam, Tamil Nadu; bottom, temple deity and consorts in procession, Kanchipuram, Tamil Nadu.
This page: top, a shop selling religious images; bottom, the Charan Paduka at Har-ki-Pauri, Uttaranchal Pradesh.

The Divine is seen in many forms: the abstract concept made concrete through a diversity of images that manifest the Godhead through beloved figures. Religious festivals like those at Banaras, Tirupati and Kumbhakonam draw together large crowds of the faithful, a time when richly-adorned deities are taken out in procession on a determined path thronged by eager pilgrims. It is also the occasion for the young to take part and learn the ways of prayer and worship.

Opp: Moments of tranquility in worship. Sadhus and acolytes pause by banks of the Ganga; pilgrims float on her waters at Banaras.

This page: The sacred fields of Hinduism are many and found throughout the country. But four are specially hallowed: Rameshwaram in the south (top left); Jagannath Puri in the east (top right); Badrinath in the north, (left); Dwarka in the west (above).

Architectural Traditions
A synthesis through ages

The magnificence of an architectural legacy, says one writer, is the definition of the greatness of a civilisation. In that respect India is country replete with gems of the built form. Because some have always been better known than others, it is only now that we are recognising the intelligent, innovative response to local conditions that constitutes the regional architecture of the people. When we look at buildings in India, large and small, we can see the enormous range and diversity of the architectural tradition.

The spatial expressions were many—the religious architecture of temple, mosque, stupa, church, gurdwara; the magnificence of monumental palaces, fortresses and mausoleums; the planned cities of Fatehpur Sikri, Jaipur and 20th century Chandigarh. The single most famous building in India is the Taj Mahal, described as 'a teardrop on the cheek of time', ethereal words for a monument in marble that is one of the wonders of the world. It features the double dome of Persian influence, where the inner dome allows for scale as the outer soars into the sky. In architecture, as in so much else, the Mughals achieved a synthesis of Islamic style and Indian workmanship that astounded the rest of the world.

pp 58-59, the sublime beauty of the Taj Mahal seen from the entrance gate.
Opp: top, Akbar's City of Victory, Fatehpur Sikri, near Agra; middle, temple amidst the ruins of Hampi, once glorious capital of the great Vijayanagara Empire, Karnataka; bottom, a view of the Kailashnath temple in Kanchipuram, Tamil Nadu.
This page: Relief carvings from one of the gates at the Buddhist stupa at Sanchi, Madhya Pradesh. The stupa as an architectural form was also hollowed out in caves.

Opp: The 8th century Shore Temple, Mahabalipuram, of the Pallava dynasty is the earliest known example of a stone-built temple in South India, and influenced later temple architecture in Tamil Nadu.
This page: top, rock-cut cave, Ajanta. The vaulted ceiling probably follows the style of earlier wooden structures. Above, the temple complex of Srirangam has a profusion of vimanas towering above the wall; the golden one indicates the main shrine.

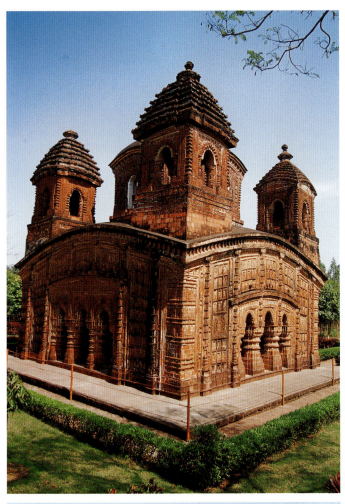

Temple construction in India varied according to characteristic regional design styles, materials and decorative devices, and we can see the diversity on these pages. **Opp:** top left, brick and terracotta temple, Vishnupur, West Bengal with typical sloping roof; bottom left, Chidambaram temple; bottom right, elaborately carved exterior of Madurai temple. **This page:** left, the soaring structure of the Thanjavur temple, top right, temple, Khajuraho; top left, exquisitely embellished Jain temple from the Dilwara complex in Mount Abu, Rajasthan. The Gol Gumbaz in Bijapur, Karnataka, (opp: top right) is the 17th century mausoleum of Adil Shah, whose central dome is second in size only to St. Peter's Basilica in Rome. A completely different architecture is seen in the Lamayuru Monastery of Ladakh (this page, above.)

Opp: top, the Napier Museum in Thiruvananthapuram, Kerala, built in the 19th century in an eclectic mix of Kerala, Mughal and Chinese influences; bottom, Humayun's Tomb, New Delhi, a World Heritage site.
This page: top, the stunning temple architecture of Somnath in Gujarat; above, ornate balcony, Jaisalmer, allowed cool breezes to flow through the building.

Royal Homes
Forts and Palaces in India

Kings and queens have been part of mythic India ; little wonder, then, that the epics and ancient tales are full of descriptions of magical palaces and mysterious fortresses. That romance can still be seen in India , and not just in Rajasthan. Through the length and breadth of the land there are royal residences of varying ages and architectural styles and to travel from one to the other is to appreciate how tastes changed over the centuries. We may marvel at the fact that some cities, like Hyderabad and Baroda (now Vadodara), had more than one palace, a marker of the opulence of former rulers.

In the south examples of magnificence abound and contrast. The Indo-Saracenic palace of Mysore is different from the elegantly simple Padmanabhapuram palace of the rulers of Travancore built in traditional Kerala style. In the north, the crumbling façade of the nine-storey Leh palace in Ladakh was said to be an inspiration for the Potala palace in Lhasa. And in the city of Lucknow—in its prime compared to St. Petersburg for splendour—the Kaiserbagh complex was originally spread over an area as large as Versailles and meticulously created as a paradise garden. Rarely was a concept as beautifully crafted or as thoroughly destroyed.

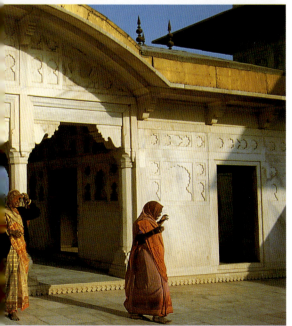

Centre: top, the Amba Vilas Palace, Mysore; middle, illuminated ruins of Golconda Fort near Hyderabad; bottom, pavilion in Agra Fort from where the Taj Mahal can be seen.
This page: above, dazzling interior of the City Palace, Jaipur.
pp 70-71, His Highness the Maharaja of Mysore performing pooja during the festival of Dussehra.

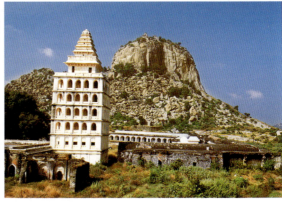
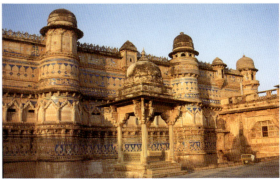

Opp: top right, interior of Umaid Bhawan Palace, Jodhpur, Rajasthan; middle, Ranjit Vilas Palace, Wankaner, Gujarat; bottom, courtyard at Uday Vilas Palace, Dungarpur. **Centre:** top, Faluknama Palace, Hyderabad; bottom, the Durbar Hall of Fateh Prakash Palace in Udaipur. **This page:** from top to bottom, interior of Faluknama Palace; Warangal Fort, Andhra Pradesh; Kalyana Mahal, Gingee; exterior of Fort, Gwalior, Madhya Pradesh.

Crafts
The skill of the artisan

Beauty speaks its own language. It is a language that the hands of the artisan know, its grammar inherited from the womb and centuries of tradition which give him mastery over his materials. The vocabulary he uses may vary in colour, texture and refinement but its end is the same: to delight the eye with skill, to add an aesthetic dimension to simple, everyday objects, to breathe life and joy into forms however temporary or short-lived the creation.

This nurtured creativity is brought to bear on an astonishing variety of materials and techniques, from the most precious of jewels and gold to humble clay, from all manner of textiles and metals to stone and straw, from painting to sculpture. In the Indian worldview all craftsmen are indeed artists, for the inborn skills of the craftsman are used to improvise as an artist. The woman bent over her embroidery creates anew as she plies her needle, adding fresh images from recent experience to her inherited repertoire. This ability to absorb and innovate enables the use of a variety of influences to create a uniquely Indian fusion. And to give birth to expressions that may differ widely, but whose encompassing meaning gives the artist's work a profound and continuing space even today.

Opp: top, unique motifs and colours of appliqué work, Orissa; bottom, ornamental bangles, Hyderabad.
This page: Telling a story in thread. Gujarati woman doing traditional embroidery.

75

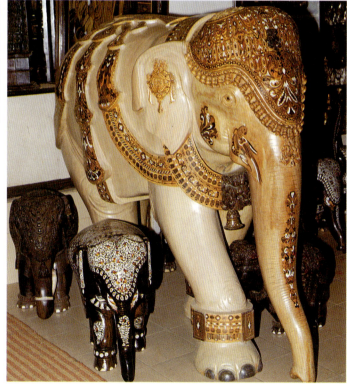

From the humblest materials to the most opulent, the hands of the artisan create a myriad beauties.
Opp: top, elaborately embellished salver; bottom left, weaving on the loom; bottom right, the exquisite art of Mughal miniature painting.
This page: top, puppets, Rajasthan; left, the potter's art; above, ivory elephant, South India.

Buddhist India
In the footsteps of the Buddha

The supreme wisdom that broke through worldly illusion, the warmth of compassion for mankind, the sage teachings of the Realised Master. These are the attributes of Gautama the Buddha, the Jewel in the Lotus Crown, whose path we follow till today, centuries after he became eternal. In India we can trace this path from Sarnath, where he preached his first sermon, through Bodh Gaya, the seat of Enlightenment, to Kushinagar where he achieved Parinirvana, sublime Immanence.

The path transcends its physicality to manifest in myriad ways. In the relief carvings of Sanchi, where his presence is evoked through images of the lotus and the Bodhi tree under whose sheltering branches he found the Way. In the Gupta sculptures where his serene face and body are perfectly stilled in meditation; in the great cave paintings of Ajanta, so filled with his humanism; in the masked dances of the monasteries of Vajrayana Buddhism, where the spiritual goodness of truth ever triumphs over evil; in the great medieval Buddhist universities schools of Nalanda and Rajgir, where the lessons were perpetuated.

Each manifestation recalls to us the Wheel of Dharma and its path of redemption: right speech, right action, right livelihood, right effort, right mindfulness, right concentration, right attitude and right view.

Centre: top, the parinirvana image at Kushinagar; middle, section of a painting from Ajanta; bottom, the Dhamek stupa at Sarnath, one of the earliest examples of extant stupa architecture.

This page: top, the Mahabodhi temple at Bodh Gaya; above, an image of the footprints of Lord Buddha, an early abstract of worship.

pp 80-81, Tibetan wall mural depicting the thousand Buddhas. Early worship of the Buddha depicted him in the abstract, as a lotus, as footprints, as the Bodhi tree, et cetera. Later, when depicted in human form, the images had stylistic variances depending on the region. In this collection of images both painted and sculpted, we can see examples from major Buddhist schools of thought, Vajrayana, Mahayana, Hinyana, from Tibet, Thailand, Sri Lanka, Japan and, of course, India.

The Faces of India
People and their lifestyles

Truly has it been written that to look at India is like an 'examination of a microcosm of the earth.' A five thousand year old civilisation embraces within itself a rare and complex diversity of peoples, cultures and traditions which have given birth to numerous ways of living, all of which co-exist in harmony. This country of more than a billion people who speak over 1600 languages and dialects is also the place where most major racial groups of the world met and mingled, turning India, as one writer says, 'into one of the greatest ethnographical museums of the world.' Here, complexions shade from the fairest to the darkest and eyes can be black, brown, green or blue. Food, language, costume and custom can vary even over short distances.

Whether tribal, rural or urban, there is one characteristic that unites the Indian people: the love of colour and ornamentation, here raised to an art form. It is evident in daily dress, whether it is the sari or one of the many kinds of turbans or a woven tribal kirtle. Brilliant reds, vibrant saffrons, ochres and greens meet bright pinks and deep blues to paint vivid images, rather like an assortment of flowers which come together in a beautiful harmony in the garden that is India.

pp 84-85, women sway in an exuberant dance. These pages: whether gathering for a fair or going about daily chores or engaged in performance art, the variety of dress and costume in India is enormous. There is a spontaneous use of colour and adornment and an unselfconscious grace in the way they are worn.

These pages and pages 90-91: Scenes from everyday India. The cycle of life continues through innocence and rites of passage, but the inherent dignity and beauty of the people, their vibrance and hope, remains.

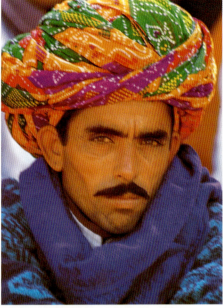

Delhi, Agra, Jaipur
The Golden Triangle

Ah, if these stones could speak, what tales they would tell! The several cities of Delhi stretching back 2,500 years in time. The palaces of Jaipur with honey-coloured forts strung like stone garlands around the surrounding hills. The exquisite beauty of Agra's monuments and the poignant splendour of Akbar's tomb at Sikandra. Through the ages they have all been mute spectators to the rise and fall of dynasties, to victories won and battles lost, to the glories of empire and the power of the people.

Within the triangle formed by these three cities lies a concentration of history spanning many centuries, a history that moulded a nation and a culture that shaped its civilisation. Between the two cities of Delhi and Agra alone, there are no less than five sites that are on UNESCO's World Heritage list: the exquisite Taj Mahal, Akbar's City of Victory (Fatehpur Sikri) and the Red Fort, all in or around Agra. And in Delhi, the Qutb Minar complex with its exquisite Islamic calligraphy in stone, and the ethereal grace of Humayun's tomb. But whether you admire these or marvel at the whimsy of the 18th century Hawa Mahal in Jaipur, you will always be reminded of why they call this the Golden Triangle.

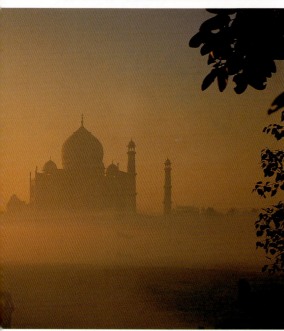

Centre: top, Republic Day illuminations make a magic spectacle of Rashtrapati Bhawan, the Presidential Palace, and government buildings in Delhi; middle, an ethereal vision, the Taj Mahal seen on a misty winter morning; bottom, the whimsical, five-storeyed façade of the Hawa Mahal in Jaipur.

This page: Qutb Minar, the Tower of Victory, built in the 12th century, is the highest historical tower in India and justly famed for the superbly calligraphed Arabic inscriptions inscribed on its red and buff sandstone.

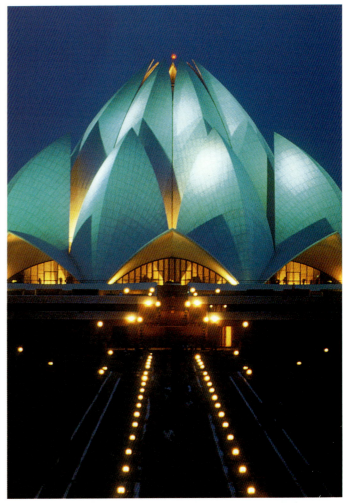

Scenes from Delhi. **Opp:** top left, colourful street bazaar; bottom left, Safdarjung's Tomb is an example of Mughal architecture on the wane; top right, the exterior of the Baha'i Temple built in the form of a blossoming lotus; bottom right, part of the exterior of the Red Fort, last seat of power of the Mughal Empire.

This page: top left, imposing India Gate commemorates the valour of soldiers who died in wars; bottom left, the historic Chandni Chowk was a mercantile street of yore; top right, the abstract lines of Jantar Mantar, an 18th century astronomical observatory.

Scenes from Agra. **Opp:** an unusual perspective of the Taj Mahal displays its perfect symmetry.
This page: top, Buland Darwaza in Fatehpur Sikri, Akbar's "City of Victory"; above, the majestic four-storied tomb of Akbar at Sikandra. Red sandstone pavilions and marble cupolas give the monument a gracious airy look.

Scenes from Jaipur. **Opp:** top, the gateway of Riddhi Siddhi Pol in the City Palace and the graceful seven-storeyed Chandra Mahal or Moon Palace; bottom, Ganesh Pol, the ceremonial gate in the Amber complex.

This page: top left, HH the Maharaja of Jaipur performing the ceremonial worship of weapons during the Dussehra festival; bottom left, the Sheesh Mahal, Amber, whose embedded mirrors sparkle like stars when the chamber is lit; above, exterior of Amber fort palace.

Kingdoms of Rajasthan
Princely India in the desert

Rajasthan—the very name means 'the place of kings'. Certainly there is not a corner of the state that does not bear the impress of the most romantic, the most royal face of India. Not surprising when you remember that at the time of Independence there were no less than nineteen princely states in the former Rajputana! And so the very air seems to sing ballads of warriors and their chivalry, and tales of valour still resound from the stones of its invincible forts and magnificent palaces. Rajasthan is often likened to a huge open-air museum where each building has its history and where the dun sands are but a backdrop for brilliantly-coloured expressions of textile art.

Travel anywhere in Rajasthan, whether to the lake city of Udaipur or the capital, Jaipur, to smaller towns and villages deep in the desert, and its regal past comes alive. Rugged fortresses perched on hilltops, elegant palaces with halls of audience, pleasure pavilions and gardens—there seems no end to the rich variety. Nothing can be more breathtaking than the magic of Jaisalmer and its fort which rises like a golden enigma from the desert. Such is the essence of the land which casts a spell of enchantment on even the most sated traveller.

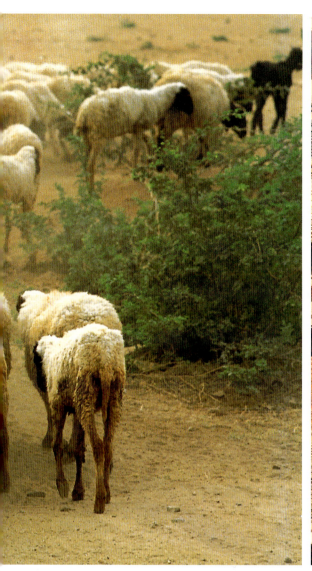

pp 100-101, patterns in the shifting sands of Jaisalmer.

Opp: top, shepherd tends to his flock, Rajasthan being the producer of 40 per cent of the country's raw wool; bottom, the elegant contours of Jaisalmer Fort rise from a hillock.

This page: exquisite stone carving is a hallmark of the havelis or mansions of the merchants of Jaisalmer.

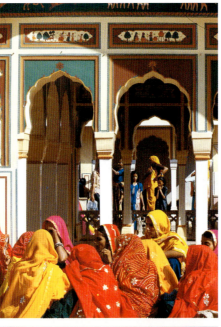

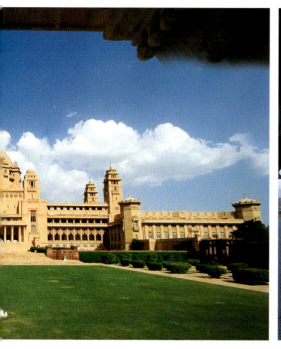

Vignettes of royal Rajasthan show sports such as elephant polo (opp: top left) and the lavish, richly-decorated interiors of palaces. It is the people who supported their kings and who engaged in the crafts for which Rajasthan is famous.

Madhya Pradesh and Khajuraho
Exploring the heart of India

Madhya Pradesh is called the heart of India, and perhaps for more reasons than its geography. For here is a kaleidoscope of the imprint of life from the earliest times to the present, an imprint that encompasses the cave paintings of Neolithic man at Bhimbetka—uncannily echoed in the roar of the tiger today at the Kanha and Bandhavgarh wildlife sanctuaries—to the built cultural heritage of Hinduism, Buddhism, Jainism and Islam. Temples, stupas, forts, palaces, sacred rivers, mountain ranges, forests: one might say that the state has everything, including the colourful histories of its former kingdoms.

And then there is the Khajuraho complex, unique in the temple architecture of India. Your heart will tell you what to make of the world-famous erotic sculptures. Perhaps you will see only the passionate physicality of bodies entwined in love. Or perhaps your eye will appreciate the wondrous skill of the sculptor's art in capturing the plasticity of the human form. Then again, you might look beyond to perceive the intention of this art: the mark of a mature civilisation inspired to build the temples as a collective ode to joyous life, to creativity and the ultimate fusion of man with his god.

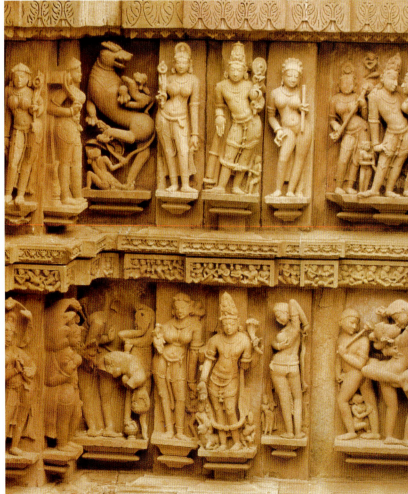

The temples of Khajuraho, built more than a thousand years ago by kings of the Chandella dynasty, are monuments to vibrant life, joy and the pleasures of love.

Centre: top, exterior view of Dauladeo temple; bottom, scultured panels from the outer wall of the Laxman temple.

This page: above, a sculpture depicts a couple imbibing wine, Laxman temple.

Opp: top, the romantic pavilions of Mandu, scene of an immortal love story; bottom, the Narmada river at Marble Rocks, Jabalpur.
This page: top, the Buddhist stupa at Sanchi; above, the unique architecture of Orchha.

Mumbai
The city of the West

When the British acquired Bombay in the 17th century as part of the dowry of the Portuguese princess, Catherine of Braganza, they could never have imagined that this string of non-descript islands would, within the space of three hundred years, become a financial nerve centre, India's 'Maximum City' as one writer has called it. Bombay, from the Portuguese Bom Baia or good bay, developed rapidly. By the 20th century it was the hub of business activities, the site of the oldest Stock Exchange in Asia and the centre of the Hindi film industry. It also changed its name to Mumbai, after the local goddess Mumbadevi.

None of this describes the frenetic energy of Mumbai, the city of dreams where millions of immigrants from the countryside came to turn their rags into riches. Some did, some failed: but all of them tried hard, spurred by the verve of a city where anything is possible. To the tourist, Mumbai is better known as an entry point for the attractions of Ajanta, Ellora and the hinterland. To the local Mumbaikar, whether he lives in a smart apartment or Asia's largest slum, it's all about the glamour of cricket and movies—and a better tomorrow.

Centre: top, the Gateway of India, built to commemorate the visit of King George V and Queen Mary in 1911; middle, the railway terminus formerly known as Victoria Terminus is a marvel of Indo-Gothic architecture; bottom, daytime view of Marine Drive.
This page: above, the Rajabhai Clock Tower, situated in the gardens of Bombay University, a fine example of the Gothic style.

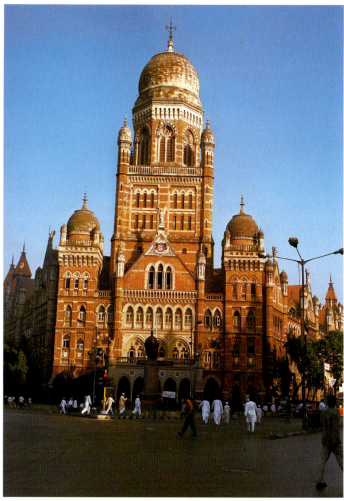
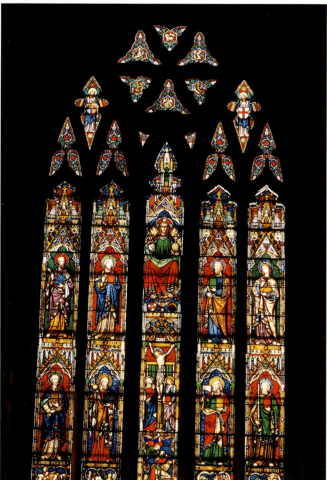

Opp: top left, the Jama Masjid or Friday mosque; top right, children enjoy a high-rise view; bottom, crowds gather to stroll on the beach.
This page: top left, the night time magic of Marine Drive, also called Queen's Necklace; top right, typical of colonial Gothic architecture; left, stained glass window from the Afghan Church, an Anglican Church named to honour the soldiers who died during the Afghan campaigns; above, the Dhobi ghat or washerman's area.

Portuguese Goa
India's playground by the sea

'Susegado' is not a word you will find in a Portuguese dictionary. It means to relax, to take life with tranquility; and it is the ambience of Goa, where a charming ease permeates a unique Indo-Iberian culture. When Alfonso Albuquerque took the area in 1510 AD, little did he realise that within the century it would thrive as a colony so beautiful and prosperous that it would become famous as Goa Dourada, Golden Goa, the Pearl of the Orient.

Today it is a prime tourist destination in India, where people flock to its forty beaches strung like garlands across 125 kilometres of coastline. Beach names like Aguada, Sinquerim, Cavelossim bear witness to the Konkani-Portuguese heritage of Goa, seen also in the many cathedrals and churches such as the Basilica of Bom Jesus, Se Cathedral and the historic seminary of Rachol, once a Muslim fortress. The Hindu heritage manifests itself temples such as the Shantadurga and Sri Manguesh. Fairs and festivals abound, from the pre-Lent carnival to the Shantadurga Prasann, a night-time procession of chariots.

Equally, the traveller can practise his own form of susegado by simply lying on a beach with a glass of feni, the fiery local spirit, and a sampler of local cuisine.

Centre: top, Vagator beach in North Goa; middle, the Se Cathedral and church of St. Francis in Old Goa lie across the square from the Basilica of Bom Jesus; bottom, sunset at Palolem beach where a few miles out you can spot dolphins.
This page: top, the splendid main altar of the Bom Jesus Basilica; above, interior of the Braganza mansion in Chandor which is over four hundred years old and has some fine carved furniture.

Elaborate embellishment marks the altars and holy points of all the older Goan churches which abound in carved and gilded images of the Son of Man and the Holy Mother. Opp: middle, detail from the chapel of the seminary at Rachol; bottom left, stained glass from the Pilar seminary; bottom right, sunrise at Dona Paula.

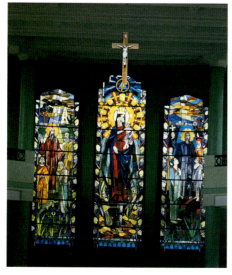

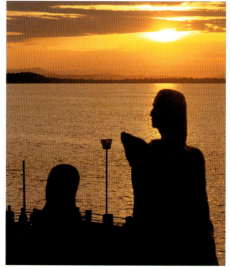

Kolkata in the East
City of Joy

Kolkata (or Calcutta, as it was once known) is one of those cities that is defined by the greatness of its people. The city itself was the creation of a 17th century agent of the British East India Company, who chose a site protected by river, creek and salt lakes; for long Calcutta was the centre of British power, the capital of Empire until 1912 with its very own memorial to Queen Victoria.

But the 'addas' of today where people gather to heatedly discuss everything over cooling cups of tea, from the state of governance to the latest football match, are symbols of the intellectual and cultural ferment that is an age-old hallmark of the city. That ferment saw the Bengal Renaissance led by thinker and reformer Raja Ram Mohan Roy, the luminous writing of Nobel prize winner Rabindranath Tagore, the compassion of Mother Teresa, the cinematic brilliance of Satyajit Ray, the inclusive spiritual vision of Sri Ramakrishna Paramhansa. Musicians, freedom fighters, polemicists, economists, novelists, scientists, visionaries and saints: all have found their place of honour in the city, and continue to. That is why no one should ever believe reports of the death of Kolkata. It is too vibrant not to live.

Opp: As unique and surreal as Kolkata itself—boats on the Hooghly river form the backdrop for the image of the Goddess Durga, ceremonially immersed at the conclusion of Pooja, Bengal's major festival.

This page: the white marble Mughal domes of the Victoria Memorial reflected in an ornamental tank. Set amidst formal gardens, it was conceived to commemorate the British Empire at its peak and formally opened in 1921.

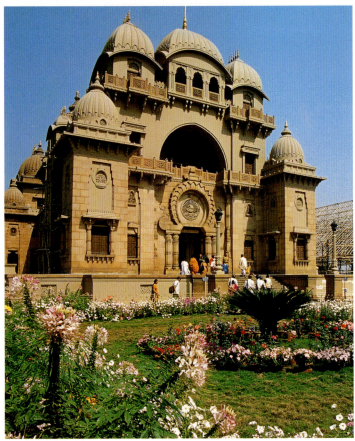

Scenes from the city. **Centre:** a view of the heart of the city. **Opp:** bottom left, Belur Math, headquarters of the Ramakrishna Mission; bottom right, Dakshineshwar temple, note its typical Bengal architecture. On either side of the Hooghly river, the two are a reminder of Sri Ramakrishna Paramhansa and his principle disciple, Swami Vivekanand.
This page: left, Goddess Durga being carried in procession; above, fruit and vegetable market.

Sun spangled Orissa
Land of the Gods

Orissa is full of surprises that delight you at every turn. Some are natural. Beautiful beaches abound on its 500 kilometers coastline. Asia's largest brackish water lake, Chilika, is a haven for birds and dolphins. The state's lush green forest cover is the habitat of a wide variety of flora and fauna, including the famed Royal Bengal Tiger. Amidst Orissa's hills and valleys nestle a number of breathtaking waterfalls and rivulets. Some are man-made—ancient monuments ranging from the ruins of Sisupalgarh to the magnificent Jagannath temple at Puri, one of Hinduism's holiest sites. The rich cultural tradition embraces with equal ease the graceful movements of classical Odissi dance and the vibrant expressions of its many tribal communities.

But surely one of the most amazing sights is the magnificent Sun Temple at Konarak, a poetic conceit frozen in stone, a 13th century monument designed in the shape of a colossal chariot drawn by seven horses bearing the Sun God, Surya, across the heavens. Breathtaking in concept as well as scale, the surface is covered with sculpture of an unsurpassed beauty and grace. No wonder, then, that the poet Rabindranath Tagore said of Konarak that 'here the language of stone surpasses the language of man'.

Chariot of the Sun God, the amazing Sun temple of Konarak stands as a magnificent monument to the skill and devotion of the Indian artist (left and above).
Centre: top, the Jagannath Puri temple.

Opp: top, intricately carved panels, Konarak, truly a medieval masterpiece; bottom, the Lingaraj temple in Bhubaneshwar is a splendid example of 11th century temple architecture in Orissa.
This page: top, the 10th century Mukteshwar temple, also in Bhubaneshwar, is smaller but perfectly proportioned and embellished with sculpted images; left, image from the chariot of the Puri Rath Yatra; above, images of Buddha at Ratnagiri.

The Secrets of Sikkim
Himalayan fastnesses

An other-worldly dimension seems to suffuse the north-eastern state of Sikkim. There is a mystical character to the clouds that waft down from the peaks, the mists that swirl across lush forests, the vast glaciers and emerald fields, the luxuriant orchids and sublimely peaceful monasteries. Dominating the landscape is the towering massif of Khangchendzonga, or Kanchenjunga, at 28,216 ft. the third highest mountain in the world. More than a mountain, Kanchenjunga is the god who watches benignly over the land.

In Gangtok, the capital, there is a constant and colourful reminder of the ethnic diversity of Sikkim that gives it such a special character. Here you see the Lepchas, the fey and gentle people who are the original inhabitants of the land. There, the Bhotias, descendents of warriors from Tibet, who became its rulers. And the Nepalese, with their brightly coloured saris and peaked caps, themselves an intriguing mix of Limbus, Rais and Chhetris.

Sikkim was once a remote Shangri-la, now within reach of the traveller. It is an enchanted and enchanting setting: a land of colours that come as much from trees and flowers as from people and costumes; of the scenic splendour of lofty mountains, lakes and rushing rivers.

Centre: top, the largest monastery in Sikkim is the Rumtek Dharma Chakra Centre of the Karma Kagyu lineage which is perched on a hilltop facing Gangtok; middle, the Sikkim Research Institute of Tibetology, a prominent research centre, houses a vast collection of rare Buddhist books, manuscripts and over 200 Buddhist icons; bottom, a profusion of chortens outside the Tashiding monastery, considered one of the holiest sites in Sikkim.
This page: above, the river Teesta.

Vignettes of Sikkim. The state flower is the Noble Orchid (dendrobium nobile); there are more than 450 orchid varieties to be found here amidst the repose of monasteries, chortens and prayer flags.

The Wonders of the South
Discovering spirit of ancient India

'Dakshin' is the Sanskrit word for 'south'. Doubtless that is the linguistic origin of Deccan, the name given to the primeval volcanic plateau that lies at the heart of South India. Separated from the North by the Vindhya mountain range, lapped by oceans on three sides, South India has an aura of tranquil timelessness supported by strong cultural roots. Its tropical climate, its forests and uplands, the lush green vegetation of the coastal areas and its architecture, culture, languages and lifestyle remain more homogenous than the variations across North India. Yet, despite apparent similarities, the four southern states of Andhra Pradesh, Karnataka, Tamil Nadu and Kerala each have a uniqueness deriving from the experiences of history and geography. The former French colony of Pondicherry and islands of Lakshwadweep are different yet again.

The thread running through South India is its tapestry of magnificent temple architecture, its splendour of handicrafts, the heritage of sandalwood, silk, rosewood and brass, and the grandeur of classical dance and music. This is as true of the countryside as of its bustling cities where the modern meets the traditional, and where the sophistication of technology and manufacture are steeped in the fragrance of flowers and the heady aroma of perfectly brewed coffee.

pp 130-131, rainbow colours illuminate the waters of Jog Falls in Karnataka.
This page: top, Brindavan Gardens near Mysore; bottom, sculptured panels from the famed medieval temple at Halebid which was once the capital of the Hoysala dynasty.
Opp: pillared and arched, the richly decorated Durbar Hall of the Mysore Palace.

pp 134-135, temple complex at Hampi, capital of the Vijayanagar Empire. **Opp:** top, 16th century church overlooks a fishing village, Kanya Kumari; bottom, train to Ooty.
This page: the richly sculpted exterior of Madurai temple.

Opp: elegant spires of the Char Minar in Hyderabad, Andhra Pradesh.
This page: the Tirumala Tirupati temple, reputedly one of the richest shrines in the world, dedicated to Lord Venkateswara.

Opp: richly caparisoned elephants are part of the cereminials at the Pooram festival at Trichur, Kerala.
This page: top, boats ply on the serene backwaters of Kerala; bottom, interior of the Vadakkumnatha temple in Trichur.

Opp: top, lush tea gardens in the rolling uplands at Munnar, Kerala; bottom, devotees offer flowers at the Sri Aurobindo Ashram in Pondicherry.

This page: Church interior, Pondicherry. Pondicherry was once the capital of the French colony in India and still bears a strong influence.

This edition
Distributed in India by

 FRONTLINE BOOKS
207,BharatChambers, 70-71, Scindia House,
Connaught Place
New Delhi 110001, India
Email : deepanfrontline@yahoo.com
© R.K. PUBLICATIONS
Introduction: Kishore Singh
Concept, layout & design Image Forte
info@imageforte.com
www.imageforte.com
Photographs © Rupinder Khullar
Text© Reeta Khullar
All rights reserved with the authors. No part of this book may be reproduced in any
form, electronically or otherwise in print, photoprint, microfilm or
in any means, without the written permission from the author.
Printed in India by: Gopsons Papers Ltd.